Medieval Tarot for Christians

Nancy Vivien Blicq

Published by Vivien Blicq, 2018.

While every precaution has been taken in the preparation of this book, the publisher assumes no responsibility for errors or omissions, or for damages resulting from the use of the information contained herein.

MEDIEVAL TAROT FOR CHRISTIANS

First edition. June 25, 2018.

ISBN: 979-8215753415

Written by Nancy Vivien Blicq.

A Guide to

Medieval Christian Tarot

For Spiritual Practice

By

Vivien Blicq

2018

Introduction

Welcome.

This study is for believers who are curious about the Tarot and for anyone who is interested in the origins of the Tarot. If you have had your cards read or watched videos of Tarot readings, you may be familiar with the modern interpretations. You may have been taught that Tarot is dangerous heresy, akin to witchcraft.

So you may be surprised as I was to learn that the Tarot has its roots in Christianity and that the cards have a deeply spiritual Christian meaning. Examined in the light of history and of scripture, the cards convey quite a different message than that which modern readers interpret.

My hope is that this book will help you to understand the cards in such a way that they will serve as a tool for reflection on your path to spiritual maturity.

Tarot was a card game that came about around the 15th century, in a place and time when the Church were the 'Powers that Be', and who for centuries had controlled nearly every aspect of life with an iron grip. It began to lose its grip with the advent of the printing press, the Protestant Reformation, and the Italian Renaissance, as people began reading the Bible for themselves, and speaking out about error in Church doctrine.

These became dangerous times to dissent. To stay in the good graces of the church, people not only had to be devoutly religious, but also be seen to be religious. Their piety can be seen in the artwork and literature of the time, in their speech and clothing, and in many aspects of their lives and behaviour, including their recreation.

So Tarot, although it is a simple game of cards, is rich with meaning. It is an allegory of the Gospel message, portrayed as the Fool's journey, in a similar way to the story of Christian in the book Pilgrim's Progress, by John Bunyan.

The cards were never intended for divination...it was a game, rather like the modern board game, 'Life', but with a Christian theme. The predecessor of modern playing cards, they may also have been used for a devotional aid, or to illustrate spiritual truths.

A word about Divination and the Occult. Occult means, 'hidden knowledge'. The word 'Arcana' (meaning mystery) was added long after the game was invented.

Unlike the nobility of 15th century Italy, who were well versed in Christian doctrine of the day, to someone who is not acquainted with scripture the illustrations on a tarot card would be a mystery. So over time various people have attached other significance to the cards, astrological archetypes, numerological, and so on. Tarot began to be used for prognostication in the 1700's.

Divination is usually thought of as seeking insight through signs and wonders, but it can also be seen as discerning the mind or will of God, not in any supernatural way, but by studying his words.

I have included scripture references, which are in keeping with the traditional meanings of the cards, and some examples of how they might apply in modern terms.

There are usually 78 cards in a modern deck, divided into Major and Minor Arcana. The original game contained only the cards of the Major Arcana. Modern decks have added astrological and numerical significance, but for the purposes of this study I will focus on the religious symbolism, commonly illustrated in the Visconti and Rider-Waite versions.

Because most people in 15th century Italy received religious instruction, such as the Catechism, the meanings of the cards were familiar themes, and the symbols and archetypes were easily understood.

Once common knowledge among the faithful of the Middle Ages, its meaning has been obscured over the centuries, so in these pages I hope to shed light on this beautiful story of faith and redemption.

From its name, Tarot, derived from the word 'Tarocchi' , which means 'Triumph', or Victory, we can derive the object of the game, which describes the sanctification process.

In the game of Tarot, as in life, we are to *have victory over* something, and that something is the self...self-will, self-gratification, self-preservation.

Here is what I will do for anyone who has victory over sin. I will let that person eat from the tree of life in God's paradise.

Revelation 2

The Major Arcana

The Fool

Enter God's kingdom through the narrow gate. The gate is large and the road is wide that leads to ruin. Many people go that way. But the gate is small and the road is narrow that leads to life. Only a few people find it.

Matthew 7.13

The Fool is the first card in the deck, and it the single most important card in the game, as you will see.

The Fool card has a numerical value of 0, and in the game it can trump all the other cards. It is a wild card, similar to the Joker in modern playing cards. It depicts a person astride a horse, leaving the broad road, and leaping over a stream into a dim forest.

In Christianity, water represents the new birth, and the stream signifies baptism, an outward expression of an inward decision. This is the period when a person is drawn to Christ, who has heard him call and followed. You may not be aware of it , but the Spirit is at work in you to lead you from the world into the kingdom of God. There comes a subtle change in the way you view the world and how you treat others as you begin to view life from a different perspective.

So why is he called 'The Fool'?

He is usually described as reckless or impulsive, and to the world he must seem so. I am reminded of the fishermen who immediately left their nets to follow Jesus.

In God's kingdom, rather than look out for ourselves, we are commanded to love, and love always requires sacrifice, of our time, or energy, or resources. From the point of view of someone who knows that everything Jesus said is true, they are perfectly sensible. But from the world's point of view, survival and success are what matters, so to an unbeliever our actions do seem foolish.

Christianity preaches the infinite worth of that which is seemingly worthless and the infinite worthlessness of that which is seemingly so valued.

Bonhoeffer

The journey is not without hazards. If you have ever walked down a narrow forest path, you know it can be difficult to see very far ahead, and to follow in someone's footsteps and not get lost, you have to be closely watching every step.

In the same way, we need to be paying close attention to Jesus's instructions so we don't get lost. He is the Way the Truth and the Life, and his path leads to eternal life. As we follow him we gradually come to trust God in every area of our lives. There may be times when we stray from the path, perhaps without realising it until we suddenly find ourselves off course.

But, here is a secret:

Because card zero is a wild card in the game of Tarrochi, you can play it at any point. so if at some point you are losing , *you can use the Fool card to get back on the path.* The journey of faith is not easy, and we all make mistakes along the way, but like the game of Tarot, and in real life, by the grace of God, we can repent and go back to the beginning and start fresh.

Some of you may be taking your first steps and some of you may have been on the path for a long while. Perhaps God is calling you to take this leap of faith, to turn away from the world and follow his Son. If you have strayed and you need to get back on the right path, these cards might help you identify areas that need a course correction.

The Magician

*The thief comes only to steal and kill and destroy. I came that they may
have life and have it abundantly.*

John 10

Up to this point, the Fool has left the broad road to follow Jesus. An exuberant leap of faith. But it is the second day of his journey, and his meagre provisions are low. He might be starting to worry about finding food and shelter as darkness falls. He might be wondering if he can really trust this Jesus, and be thinking of turning back.

This is where things start to get interesting. He is about to meet his first character on this path, and he is a sly fox.

The card usually portrays a man in ecclesiastical robes, standing at a table covered in symbols of the four elements, (which are represented by suits in the Minor Arcana), which he appears to invoke with the wand in his hand.

In modern Tarot, the Magician is portrayed as a benevolent guide, but he might more accurately be described as the personification of self-preservation.

Early in his ministry, Jesus was tempted by the devil, so it seems fitting that the first person the Fool meets with on his journey is the Magician. The Magician offers food and shelter and security and happiness, and right about now The Fool is pretty hungry. There is just one catch...

*...the devil took him to a very high mountain and showed him all the
kingdoms of the world and their glory. And he said to him, "All these I will
give you, if you will fall down and worship me.*

Matthew 4

He lays in wait for new believers, and is deceitful. Jesus called him the Prince of the World, and the Father of Lies.

Now the serpent was more crafty than any other beast of the field that the Lord God had made.

Genesis 3

Jesus spoke of this in the parable of the sower and the seeds...

Listen then to what the parable of the sower means: When anyone hears the message about the kingdom and does not understand it, the evil one comes and snatches away what was sown in their heart. This is the seed sown along the path.

Matthew 13

Until now the Fool has been master of his own destiny...striving for survival, using his strength and will to sustain him, but now he has pledged himself to Jesus. The lesson in this card is that there is only one path to God.

This new path may lead you to suffering or persecution, as it did the early believers. You may not literally hang on a cross, but you may make many sacrifices along the way for love. Jesus was persecuted and died on the cross, and he said that the servant is not greater than the master.

Modern readers interpret this card as having to do with manifesting. To some extent you are the master of your own destiny, in a minute way perhaps, on the grand scale, but also in a profound eternal way. You are free to choose your path, and God wouldn't have it any other way. However much or little we are influenced by the changing positions of the cosmos and other factors, we are free to make decisions in our lives that affect ourselves and others. We can manipulate our circumstances in such a way as to bring about a desired goal, but we are responsible for the outcome.

For what is a man profited, if he shall gain the whole world, and lose his own soul? or what shall a man give in exchange for his soul?

Mark 8

Much of what we have thought of as magic in the past, was just specialised knowledge. To know the properties of plants, for example, was information that was passed down in families over generations, and perhaps not generally understood. Sometimes that which is not understood is feared for its power and inherent threat, when it ought be treasured. Revered, or thought to be God-given, when it is not. So we can easily delude others into thinking that we have special powers, even when we haven't. And we can wield considerable power and influence over others in this way, to our own ends, be it glory, or financial gain.

There is lots of snake oil out there. So in your life the Magician might be some false teaching masquerading as spiritual truth. Who is to say whether this prophetess or that teacher is the real thing or a fraud? It is hard to know. Only time will tell if their predictions are right, and by then most of them will have been long gone with your money. There is also an element of self-fulfilling prophecy. If I tell you that you are going to have a miserable day, it is probable that you will go about having a miserable day. Psych 101. And we all want so much to have something to believe in...some higher power to help us, and heal us and give us what we need and want. Preferably with no strings attached. And depending on how deluded we are, one that can be manipulated.

We don't want to do God's will...we want God to do our will.

Maybe it is well to be reminded at the outset that we are not following this path to achieve our own ends, but God's, by his power. Make no mistake.. unlike the master of manipulation, the Prince of the World, who can only lie and deceive, this is real power. But it is to be carefully wielded in the cause of righteousness, and until we have the spiritual maturity to make decisions based on love and in line with the will of God, we will not be trusted with it. We can do nothing without him, Jesus said.

But with him, we can effect real and lasting change in the world, partly in miraculous ways, by divine intervention, but largely through our mundane daily lives, by following his example and instructions to love the Lord your God with all your heart, mind and strength, and to love one another. That is the when the real magic happens.

You don't need any magic tricks to connect with God. He is aware of every minute detail of your life, even to the number of hairs on your head. And He wants you to live in health, in peace and harmony, free of suffering or sorrow. The way there is not through manipulating the world, but by choosing to trust God, who has your best interests at heart and who is willing and able to intervene in your life for good, and by following the steps of his Son along the path, one step at a time. There are no shortcuts.

Test the spirits. If someone advertises any other spiritual path, don't believe it.

Jesus said, "I am the Way and the Truth and the Life. No one can go to the Father except by Me.

John 14

The High Priestess

*But the Helper, the Holy Spirit, whom the Father will send in my name, he
will teach you all things and bring to your remembrance all that I have
said to you.*

John 14

UP TO THIS POINT, THE Fool has made a decision to follow Jesus,
and has met with the deceiver, and has escaped him . Before he goes any
farther he needs some guidance so that he doesn't fall prey, and this is
where the High Priestess comes in. She shares with him the secret to
overcoming, to aid him on his journey.

In traditional decks, the High Priestess is portrayed as a woman, seated
between two pillars at the entrance to a temple, which are inscribed with
letters, and she is holding a scroll that has the word Tora (Torah or Law)
written on it.

She represents Purity and a life of serving God and upholding the Word
(truth).

We find the meaning of the pillars in 2 Chronicles and in 2 Kings.
The letters B and J, stand for Boaz, which means 'Strength', and Jachin,
which means 'Establish in the Lord'. Together it means to be 'strongly
established in the Lord'.

The key here is to read the words of Jesus. You don't have to memorise
the whole Bible, but you do need to know what Jesus said. He said
that the Spirit will remind you of his words when you need them, and

some of you reading will have found this to be true. Whenever you need guidance, a phrase that Jesus said will come to mind.

Sometimes when we have a problem, our instinct for self preservation will cause us to react in fear. At such times we might forget that God has a plan, and go back to our old way of thinking.

They say that if you ever get lost in the forest, stop right where you are and don't panic or go running off in all directions. The same applies to our spiritual lives. If you find yourself in a dilemma, stop right there and ask for guidance. If you have read his words, he will remind you clearly and show you the way forward. They are your map.

If you draw this card it is a reminder that you have been given a powerful lifeline that will aid you on the rest of your journey. Whatever you are going through, whatever challenges you are facing, he has given you the means to navigate.

"Everyone then who hears these words of mine and does them will be like a wise man who built his house on the rock.

Matthew 7

The Empress and Emperor

IN THE TIME WHEN TAROT originated, it was thought that government leaders were appointed by God to rule, under the authority of the Church. So it is not surprising to find them here at the top of the heap, perhaps in deference to the rulers of the day.

The Empress is portrayed as a benevolent monarch, who cares for her subjects, and rules with love and concern for the wellbeing of everyone under her protection. But she also holds the power of life and death over her subjects, and is to be feared and respected.

The Emperor represents her male counterpart, with the power to advance or demolish, but where the Empress is seen as a benevolent provider, the Emperor represents the strong paternal protector. Together they represent a kingdom of peace and plenty, free from oppression or want.

In modern terms you might view them as a fair and just government that looks out for the safety and wellbeing of everyone under its protection. Taxes, healthcare, justice, trade, defense..these are weighty matters, and decisions made with the stroke of a pen can affect the lives of thousands of people for good or ill.

If you live in a democracy, and are able to vote, you bear responsibility for the government you elect and their policies, so vote for the best interests of all, not for self interest. Where people go without food or housing or education or medical care, or where there is corruption, nepotism, injustice, it is not a prosperous or well managed kingdom, and is not in keeping with God's mandate. If you live under a corrupt or oppressive regime, your life might be a miserable one.

All of us are subject to world authorities, but for believers, the final authority is God. And those of us who hold positions of power and influence are commanded to do justice and love mercy, so we have a responsibility to govern accordingly.

Here is where the Fool learns that unlike the secular world, in God's kingdom we are called to serve, not to be served.

But Jesus called them together and said, "You know that the rulers in this world lord it over their people, and officials flaunt their authority over those under them. But among you it will be different. Whoever wants to be a leader among you must be your servant

Matthew 20

The Hierophant

"Well did Isaiah prophesy of you hypocrites, as it is written,

"'This people honors me with their lips,

but their heart is far from me;

in vain do they worship me,

teaching as doctrines the commandments of men.'

Mark 7

THE FOOL WILL NEED discernment for this next part, because the next person he meets in the Tarot, is the Hierophant. This is where the lifeline that he got from the High Priestess is important..

The Hierophant is portrayed as a religious authority, someone who enforces the rules of the Church. In some cards there are two lesser ministers kneeling in submission before him. This card represents dogma and doctrine and is sometimes called The Pope card.

As the saying from that time, 'give me a child for the first seven years and I will give you the man', people were indoctrinated from an early age and did not challenge the authority of the Church. During that period in history the Church committed some acts of cruelty and many denominations were born in reaction to doctrinal error, some as misguided as the one they escaped from.

It can be difficult for a seeker to know which , if any, have the truth. And if we sit under the teaching of only one pastor or denomination for many years we may only be seeing through a narrow lens.

So the lesson in the Hierophant card is to examine everything you are taught, and observe their actions.

"Be on your guard against false religious teachers, who come to you dressed up as sheep but are really greedy wolves. You can tell them by their fruit. Do you pick a bunch of grapes from a thorn-bush or figs from a clump of thistles?

Matthew 7

If something you are taught doesn't line up with the words of Jesus, discard it. Just because your seminary or church leadership teaches something, does not mean that it is from God. Even the structure of the church has long been modeled after the top-down organisational style of the world, and is not in keeping with what Jesus ordained.

In the body of Christ, as they say, the ground is level at the foot of the cross. It is a wonderful thing when believers come together to minister to others, but it can also devolve into a mutual admiration society. Going to seminary does not automatically make someone a better Christian, nor do letters after their name make them any more spiritual than anyone else. In fact Jesus warned us that whoever does not receive the kingdom of God like a child, will not enter it.

What you believe will influence your actions. Issues like scriptural inerrancy, and the trinity, matter. Remember that the Bible is a compilation of historical documents, prophecy, poetry, and letters from various believers. The bottom line is, if any doctrine is not in harmony with the exact words of Jesus, discard it. Even if it is in the Bible.

There are teachers who do an end run around the truth by misusing the Bible, and many of us have been taken in by false doctrine, even in some of the the most conservative denominations. We accept what is told to us without question because the person telling us is supposed to be an authority. But what we call the church looks nothing like what Jesus prayed for, so be careful what you hear. Truth can bear examination, as they say. Jesus said that he was careful to say only that which his Father instructed him, so his words are our doctrinal watermark. This is why you need to know what he actually said, so that you will recognise counterfeit teaching.

So before he goes rushing off to prosyletise all over the place, the Fool might be advised to first be sure that he is walking the walk. Jesus did not tell us to stand on corners with placards rebuking people for their sins. He did tell us to live a sinless life. When you have done that you will be in a position to guide others, but until then we are called only to treat others as we wish to be treated, with compassion and dignity. So if you are a new believer, practice quiet anonymous love for a while before you start advertising. If you are walking in love, people will be attracted without you saying a word. God will do the rest.

..you have hidden these things from the wise and learned, and revealed them to children..

Matthew 11

He who has an ear, let him hear what the Spirit says to the churches. To the one who conquers I will grant to eat of the tree of life, which is in the paradise of God.

Revelation 1

The Lovers

So they are no longer two but one flesh. What therefore God has joined together, let not man separate.

Matthew 19

Here the Fool meets with what some call the testing ground of our faith. Certainly marriage can be said to be a perfect setting for learning love and self-sacrifice.

The Lovers card depicts a man and woman, and above them a winged angelic being. It represents the sacrament of marriage, a joyful union, blessed by God. The image of the triangle is analogous for a healthy marriage, with God at the top, and each person drawing support from God individually, so that they in turn are able to strengthen one another.

In 15th century Italy, marriage was a big deal. Holy Matrimony. The Church espoused marriage and procreation as a path to sanctification, and the secular world viewed it as a way to ensure a stable society. Marriages were arranged for political expediency akin to corporate mergers, and weddings were elaborate celebrations. It was a patriarchal society where women were valued by dowry and were thought to be saved by bearing children. Marriage was considered indissoluble.

Throughout the Bible, God has strong words concerning marriage and divorce, and we are to honor our commitment to each other. In God's eyes we are no longer two separate people, but one unit. This card can also represent communion with other believers or the church as the bride of Christ.

The Chariot

---

*I was hungry and you gave Me food; I was thirsty and you gave Me drink;
I was a stranger and you took Me in; I was naked and you clothed Me; I
was sick and you visited Me; I was in prison and you came to Me.'*

Matthew 25

THE CHARIOT CARD DEPICTS a man driving a chariot drawn by two horses. It is an illustration of faith in action.

Now the Fool is called to minister to others, in tangible ways. The Catechism of Trent in 1566 defined these as acts of corporal mercy. To alleviate human suffering, including injustice, poverty, deprivation, oppression and sickness.

In modern terms when I see this card I am reminded of aid workers who go to foreign countries to help people in crisis. Disaster relief, sanctuary for refugees, hospitals, shelters and food banks are all examples of love in action.

Also soldiers, firefighters and policemen who risk their lives to protect us.

This can also been seen as the role of the church as the body of Christ. The reason we gather is not just to sing hymns and listen to a sermon. We come together to go out into the community to help people. The church is meant to be a sanctuary for those in need- a shelter for the homeless, a safe refuge.

These are also the small quiet acts of kindness..the person who visits a sick neighbour, or takes a moment to hold a door for someone. The smallest act of charity can speak more loudly than the most eloquent words.

Justice

———

and what does the Lord require of you but to do justice, and to love kindness, and to walk humbly with your God?

Micah 6

Justice is illustrated by a seated woman holding a pair of scales. She personifies the qualities of wisdom, fairness, equality, and balance. Justice is one of four Cardinal Virtues, together with Strength, Temperance and Purity.

If you draw this card, think about where in your society there might be injustice. Do your laws discriminate against someone? Perhaps you have been unfair toward someone, or maybe you have suffered an injustice.

For judgment without mercy will be shown to anyone who has not been merciful. Mercy triumphs over judgment.

James 2

If you are someone with the power to administer justice, do so prayerfully and impartially, remembering that you will also be judged with the same measure.

the Lord seeth not as man seeth; for man looketh on the outward appearance, but the Lord looketh on the heart.

1 Samuel 16

For with what judgment ye judge, ye shall be judged: and with what measure ye mete, it shall be measured to you again.

Matthew 7

The Hermit

And he said unto them, Come ye apart into the wilderness, and rest a while..

Mark 6

THE HERMIT CARD DEPICTS a man travelling alone at night in a deserted place, with a lamp to guide him.

This card represents a time of retreat, for study, prayer and reflection. It may also refer to the monastic life. In those days there were many monastic orders, for men and women. Some lived in communities and others lived as hermits, in solitude.

Like Elijah in the desert after his victory, in spite of having overcome many challenges, perhaps the Fool is feeling overwhelmed and depleted of energy.

Elijah walked for a whole day into the desert. He sat down under a bush and asked to die. "I have had enough, Lord," he prayed.

1 Kings 19

Jesus also went off by himself on occasion, for a time of solitude, to be in communion with the Father.

Sometimes the small still voice can't be heard in the bustle of everyday life, and we all need to be alone for a little while, even if it is just a few hours a week. Maybe you need a time of refreshing, a renewal of the body and spirit. Or a time for grieving and for healing.

He maketh me to lie down in green pastures: he leadeth me beside the still waters.

Psalm 23

The Wheel

IN THIS CARD, THE FOOL experiences a life changing revelation of God's power and presence.

In traditional decks, the card shows a wheel within a wheel, and on it images of the winged creatures described in Ezekiel's vision of God's throne. These same creatures are also mentioned in the Revelation as the angels who hold back the four corners of the world.

Each of the four had the face of a human being, and on the right side each had the face of a lion, and on the left the face of an ox; each also had the face of an eagle Ezekiel 1

Some readers interpret this card as representing Karma- the belief that we live through many incarnations, and that how you behave in this one will determine how you spend the next. For example, they believe that a person born into poverty is being punished for some misdeed in a previous incarnation, and that to help them is to interfere with God's punishment. Saying that a person's suffering is meant to teach them a lesson is a convenient way to rationalise our refusal to love. We only want to help people we like or those we deem deserving. But as believers we are not to condemn, we are to have mercy... to reach down and help them up, like the good Samaritan.

The real meaning of this card is not in the image of the wheels, but in the message that God gave Ezekiel when he promised a time of reckoning when those who were faithful would be restored, and their unjust rulers be punished. It is a reminder that God hears the cries of the suffering.

Strength

For whatsoever is born of God overcometh the world: and this is the victory that overcometh the world, even our faith.

1 John 5

In this card, the Fool is being called upon to stand his ground. Perhaps in helping others, he has taken a moral stand in defense of some righteous cause and has met with opposition.

I know thy works: behold, I have set before thee an open door, and no man can shut it: for thou hast a little strength, and hast kept my word, and hast not denied my name.

Revelation 3

Strength is the second of the four Cardinal Virtues, that were part of the teachings of the church during the Middle Ages, together with Temperance, Justice and Purity. The card is also called Courage or Fortitude, and it depicts a woman subduing a lion.

Augustine of Hippo described them thusly:

*For these four virtues (would that all felt their influence in their minds as they have their names in their mouths!), I should have no hesitation in defining them: that temperance is love giving itself entirely to that which is loved; **fortitude is love readily bearing all things for the sake of the loved object**; justice is love serving only the loved object, and therefore ruling rightly; prudence is love distinguishing with sagacity between what hinders it and what helps it. (De moribus eccl., Chap. xv)*

In the previous chapter I spoke about love in action. Sometimes love means speaking out against wrongdoing or injustice on someone's behalf. If you take a moral stand in defense of some principle, you may well encounter opposition, or even persecution.

In this card I am reminded of the story of Elijah, when he went up against the prophets of Baal. He stood quietly while they screamed and yelled and cut themselves to try and get their god to make the wood catch fire. When it was his turn, Elijah said a simple prayer. And then all hell broke loose. Elijah wasn't especially strong, but he was strong in his faith that God could and would answer his request. Faith as tiny as a mustard seed.

Fear thou not; for I am with thee: be not dismayed; for I am thy God: I will strengthen thee; yea, I will help thee; yea, I will uphold thee with the right hand of my righteousness.

Isaiah 41

Love the Lord your God with all your heart and with all your soul and with all your mind and with all your strength.

Mark 12

This card is to encourage us to stand firm in trusting God, no matter what. When we know that God has our backs, like Elijah, and like the woman of Proverbs, we can meet every crisis with confidence and calm serenity.

Strength and honour are her clothing; and she shall rejoice in time to come.
Proverbs 31

These things I have spoken unto you, that in me ye might have peace. In the world ye shall have tribulation: but be of good cheer; I have overcome the world.

John 16

The Hanged Man

... he who does not take his cross and follow after Me is not worthy of Me. He who finds his life will lose it, and he who loses his life for My sake will find it.

Matthew 10

This card depicts a man hanging from a beam by one foot, which was a punishment for heresy and other crimes, in 15th century Italy. It may have served as a reminder of the consequences for disobeying the church authorities, during the counter-reformation. It was believed that torture would bring about repentance, or conversion. For the purpose of this study I am assigning it a different meaning. This card symbolises persecution and self-sacrifice.

Love always requires sacrifice, of our time, energy or resources. For example, giving someone your last loaf of bread means that you might go without. It might mean returning love for hatred or being patient and kind to someone who is difficult. Your every loving action is a living sacrifice.

Blessed are you when they revile and persecute you, and say all kinds of evil against you falsely for My sake. Rejoice and be exceedingly glad, for great is your reward in heaven, for so they persecuted the prophets who were before you.

Matthew 5

Jesus replied, "The hour has come for the Son of Man to be glorified. Very truly I tell you, unless a kernel of wheat falls to the ground and dies, it remains only a single seed. But if it dies, it produces many seeds. Anyone who loves their life will lose it, while anyone who hates their life in this world will keep it for eternal life. Whoever serves me must follow me; and where I am, my servant also will be. My Father will honor the one who serves me.

John 12

There may come a time in your life when you experience persecution or hardship because of your faith. Endure.

And they overcame him by the blood of the Lamb, and by the word of their testimony; and they loved not their lives unto the death.

Revelation 12

Death

I am the resurrection and the life. He who believes in Me, though he may die, he shall live. And whoever lives and believes in Me shall never die.

John 11

The Death card depicts a rider on a pale horse, from John's prophetic vision. This is death personified.

And I looked, and behold a pale horse: and his name that sat on him was Death

Revelation 6

Here the Fool, perhaps sick or injured, has had a brush with death and become aware of his fragile mortality. Or maybe has lost a loved one.

Death is the one thing that all of us fear. In some ancient decks the card is not named, and modern card readers often present this card as meaning change or impermanence, so as not to scare the querent. Although Tarot cards cannot predict death, they can remind us that by the sacrifice of his son, God has delivered us from the fear of death, and promised eternal life.

Forasmuch then as the children are partakers of flesh and blood, he also himself likewise took part of the same; that through death he might destroy him that had the power of death, that is, the devil;

And deliver them who through fear of death were all their lifetime subject to bondage.

Hebrews 2

There is a presently a limit on our years, but in heaven it will not be so. You will have consciousness and remember this life. You will look back upon this time as a sort of preliminary entrance exam.

If you draw this card, you needn't be afraid of it...it is a reminder that you are loved eternally.

And God shall wipe away all tears from their eyes; and there shall be no more death, neither sorrow, nor crying, neither shall there be any more pain: for the former things are passed away.

Revelation 21

Yea, though I walk through the valley of the shadow of death, I will fear no evil: for thou art with me

Psalm 23

Temperance

Behold, I have refined thee, but not as silver; I have chosen thee in the furnace of affliction.

Isaiah 48

Temperance is the fourth of the cardinal virtues. It is personified by a woman pouring water from one jug into another. Tempering is a process in which a substance is modified, through heat or other means. Chocolate is tempered to make it smooth, for example.

Temperance is moderation in conduct, by exercising patience, kindness, gentleness and self-control. As you learn to walk in love you are being refined. You are becoming a vessel of God's love, poured out to others.

Love is patient and kind; love does not envy or boast; it is not arrogant or rude. It does not insist on its own way; it is not irritable or resentful;it does not rejoice at wrongdoing, but rejoices with the truth. Love bears all things, believes all things, hopes all things, endures all things. Love never ends.

1 Corinthians 13

My dear brothers and sisters, take note of this: Everyone should be quick to listen, slow to speak and slow to become angry, because human anger does not produce the righteousness that God desires.

James 1

The Devil

———

The one who does what is sinful is of the devil, because the devil has been sinning from the beginning. The reason the Son of God appeared was to destroy the devil's work.

1 John 3

I n this card, the Devil is shown with horns and hooves, with people in chains before him. This was a common representation in the artwork of the day, in the paintings of Hieronymous Bosch depicting the Seven Deadly Sins, for example, which was a concept being taught by the church at that time.

Most people were illiterate in those days, and those who were not, had largely been educated by the church. So such paintings were a way of teaching spiritual lessons to people who could not read.

In this card the lesson was that if we succumb to sin (like pride, greed, lust, sloth, envy, gluttony and wrath), we will be taken captive by the devil. Here the Fool is warned to beware of temptation. As James warned in his letter:

Blessed is the man who endures temptation; for when he has been approved, he will receive the crown of life which the Lord has promised to those who love Him. Let no one say when he is tempted, "I am tempted by God"; for God cannot be tempted by evil, nor does He Himself tempt anyone. But each one is tempted when he is drawn away by his own desires and enticed. Then, when desire has conceived, it gives birth to sin; and sin, when it is full-grown, brings forth death.

James 1

We have an enemy. But believers also have power and authority over all the power of the enemy.

And the great dragon was cast out, that old serpent, called the Devil, and Satan, which deceiveth the whole world: he was cast out into the earth, and his angels were cast out with him.

And I heard a loud voice saying in heaven, Now is come salvation, and strength, and the kingdom of our God, and the power of his Christ: for the accuser of our brethren is cast down, which accused them before our God day and night.

And they overcame him by the blood of the Lamb, and by the word of their testimony; and they loved not their lives unto the death.

Revelation 12

The Tower

———

The Tower card illustrates calamity, or destruction. The earliest decks showed a tower being destroyed in a storm.

Jesus spoke of our faith being tested in the same way that if a house is built on rock it can withstand storms. This could mean anything, from sickness to financial collapse. If our lives have been lived trusting and depending on God, we will have a strong foundation, and keep obeying him even if bad things happen. Jesus warned that in the last days, many people will fall away when their survival is threatened. We will find some examples of trusting God in the storms of life as we explore the Minor Arcana.

"Therefore whoever hears these sayings of Mine, and does them, I will liken him to a wise man who built his house on the rock: and the rain descended, the floods came, and the winds blew and beat on that house; and it did not fall, for it was founded on the rock.

"But everyone who hears these sayings of Mine, and does not do them, will be like a foolish man who built his house on the sand: and the rain descended, the floods came, and the winds blew and beat on that house; and it fell. And great was its fall."

Matthew 7

The Star

The heavens declare the glory of God; and the firmament sheweth his handywork. Psalm 19

This card depicts a bright star in the night sky. Modern decks also show a woman pouring water from a jug.

Around the time when Tarot became popular, astronomy was coming into vogue, and in 1647 William Lilly published his book, Christian Astrology. The Sun, Moon and Star cards may have been added during that period. Later, in 1882, Joseph Seiss published The Gospel in the Stars, showing a correlation between the constellations and the gospel story.

The Star card can be seen as a representation of heaven and the promise of eternal life. This is the card of Hope.

He determines the number of the stars; he gives to all of them their names.

Psalm 147

And beware lest you raise your eyes to heaven, and when you see the sun and the moon and the stars, all the host of heaven, you be drawn away and bow down to them and serve them, things that the Lord your God has allotted to all the peoples under the whole heaven.

Deuteronomy 4

And a great sign appeared in heaven: a woman clothed with the sun, with the moon under her feet, and on her head a crown of twelve stars.

Revelation 12

The Moon

The Moon card is generally said to represent things revealed that were hidden, or the emotions. Astrologically it is associated with the sign of Cancer, and modern illustrations usually depict a crab.

The moon can be said to have a profound influence on our lives, both on our planet and our bodies. I interpret this card in two ways. First, as a caution, to not let our actions be dictated by our emotions, which can be changeable, and secondly, to remind us of God's promises in a time of darkness.

In his days shall the righteous flourish; and abundance of peace so long as the moon endureth.

Psalm 72

The Sun

I am the light of the world: he that followeth me shall not walk in darkness, but shall have the light of life.

John 8

The Sun card is symbolic of Jesus Christ, the triumphant savior. He brings spiritual light to a world in darkness. He was the first person to overcome, and to show us the path to eternal life.

Think about the how the Sun provides life-giving energy and warmth, and how a tiny flame dispels darkness.

Plants can't live without light, and in the same way we will wither spiritually if we are not close to the light of Jesus. Spend time in his presence. Read his words and be sensitive to the promptings of the Spirit.

Then Jesus said unto them, Yet a little while is the light with you. Walk while ye have the light, lest darkness come upon you: for he that walketh in darkness knoweth not whither he goeth.

John 12

And the light shineth in darkness; and the darkness comprehended it not...That was the true Light, which lighteth every man that cometh into the world.

John 1

And I saw heaven opened, and behold a white horse; and he that sat upon him was called Faithful and True, and in righteousness he doth judge and make war.

*His eyes were as a flame of fire, and on his head were many crowns;
and he had a name written, that no man knew, but he himself.*

*And he was clothed with a vesture dipped in blood: and his name is
called The Word of God.*

Judgement

The Judgement card shows an angel, blowing a trumpet, and the dead being resurrected. This is an illustration of the last judgement, when everyone will be judged according to their words and actions. Just as in the parable of the ten virgins, we are to be found ready and living in holiness at all times, because he will come unexpectedly.

If Jesus came right now, would you be found living in righteousness?

This card is a call to examine ourselves, to see if we are living in accordance with his commandment.

When the Son of man shall come in his glory, and all the holy angels with him, then shall he sit upon the throne of his glory:

And before him shall be gathered all nations: and he shall separate them one from another, as a shepherd divideth his sheep from the goats:

And he shall set the sheep on his right hand, but the goats on the left.

Then shall the King say unto them on his right hand, Come, ye blessed of my Father, inherit the kingdom prepared for you from the foundation of the world:

For I was an hungred, and ye gave me meat: I was thirsty, and ye gave me drink: I was a stranger, and ye took me in:

Naked, and ye clothed me: I was sick, and ye visited me: I was in prison, and ye came unto me.

Then shall the righteous answer him, saying, Lord, when saw we thee an hungred, and fed thee? or thirsty, and gave thee drink?

*When saw we thee a stranger, and took thee in? or naked, and clothed
thee?*

Or when saw we thee sick, or in prison, and came unto thee?

*And the King shall answer and say unto them, Verily I say unto you,
Inasmuch as ye have done it unto one of the least of these my brethren, ye
have done it unto me.*

*Then shall he say also unto them on the left hand, Depart from me, ye
cursed, into everlasting fire, prepared for the devil and his angels:*

*For I was an hungred, and ye gave me no meat: I was thirsty, and ye gave
me no drink:*

*I was a stranger, and ye took me not in: naked, and ye clothed me not: sick,
and in prison, and ye visited me not.*

*Then shall they also answer him, saying, Lord, when saw we thee an
hungred, or athirst, or a stranger, or naked, or sick, or in prison, and did
not minister unto thee?*

*Then shall he answer them, saying, Verily I say unto you, Inasmuch as ye
did it not to one of the least of these, ye did it not to me.*

*And these shall go away into everlasting punishment: but the righteous
into life eternal.*

Matthew 24

---

*I saw a great white throne, and him that sat on it, from whose face the
earth and the heaven fled away; and there was found no place for them.*

*And I saw the dead, small and great, stand before God; and the books were
opened: and another book was opened, which is the book of life: and the*

dead were judged out of those things which were written in the books, according to their works.

And the sea gave up the dead which were in it; and death and hell delivered up the dead which were in them: and they were judged every man according to their works.

Revelation 21

The World

'*Well done, good and faithful servant! You have been faithful with a few things; I will put you in charge of many things. Come and share your master's happiness!*'

Matthew 25

THIS IS THE LAST CARD in the Major arcana, and it symbolises the triumph of the Fool over sin . He has overcome the world and its desires, to do the will of God, and now he will obtain his reward.

This is the victory that has overcome the world, even our faith. Who is it that overcomes the world? Only the one who believes that Jesus is the Son of God.

1 John 5

He that overcometh shall inherit all things; and I will be his God, and he shall be my son.

Revelation 21

The Minor Arcana

Introduction

Where the Major Arcana represents the main lessons in life, the Minor Arcana deals with the details. They can work together to illustrate lessons for daily living.

There are four suits, and each includes 4 court cards, page, knight, queen and king.

In the hierarchy of the Middle Ages, knights were something like private security forces, who served the King and Queen. They were highly trained warriors, who lived by a code of chivalry, and held to the highest moral standards.

Pages were young boys of nobility, who served the knights ,while themselves being trained as future knights.

The early cards of the Minor Arcana were simple, numerical illustrations, and probably had no allegorical significance attached to them. It wasn't until around the 1700's, when the designs began to have a astrological theme.

As with the Major cards, each suit can be seen as a progression of challenges leading to spiritual maturity, beginning with the Ace, and ending with the Court cards.

Swords

For the word of God is living and active. Sharper than any double-edged sword, it pierces even to dividing soul and spirit, joints and marrow. It is able to judge the thoughts and intentions of the heart.

Hebrews 4

The suit of swords represents discernment. This is where we begin to understand things from God's point of view, and apply that wisdom to our daily lives. This is critical thinking, and logic.

Ace of Swords

THIS CARD DEPICTS A hand coming from the clouds, holding a sword. It signifies God given understanding, or the spirit of discernment. Spiritual enlightenment, or insight, to perceive people or situations through the lens of Jesus's teaching and example.

Together with a Major card, it could signify needing spiritual discernment in that area. In combination with the Magician card, for example, it could mean needing discernment to recognise false teaching. *'by their fruits you will know them'. (Matthew 7)*

Two of Swords

THIS CARD SHOWS A BLINDFOLDED woman holding two crossed swords.

Here the Fool is being asked to make a decision, not based on his own judgement, but on the standards that Jesus has set out.

In combination with the Chariot card, for example, it could indicate needing wisdom in serving others or supporting a cause.

Trust in the Lord with all your heart and lean not on your own understanding.

Proverbs 3

Three of Swords

THE CARD SHOWS AN IMAGE of a heart being pierced by three swords. It can mean unrequited love, or a loving action that has resulted in personal loss, rejection or heartache.

Together with the Justice card, for example, it could mean that you are being asked to make a fair decision even if it comes at a cost to you.

Do not think that I came to bring peace on earth. I did not come to bring peace but a sword. For I have come to set a man against his father, a daughter against her mother, and a daughter-in-law against her mother-in-law; and a man's enemies will be those of his own household.

Matthew 10

Four of Swords

I CALL THIS CARD, THE knight resting. It shows a knight lying peacefully on his tomb, his swords close by.

This suggests someone who is learning to pray and wait upon God for inspiration. Or, to take an action and then leave the outcome with God, not knowing how it will turn out, but trusting that God has it in hand.

With the Moon card, for example, it could mean praying for clarity about a situation that you don't have all the facts about, and then calmly waiting and listening for God to answer.

Five of Swords

THIS CARD SHOWS A MAN holding three swords, with two others who have laid down their swords. It represents opposition, arguments or debate.

If, for example, this card is in combination with the Hierophant card, it could mean challenging some wrongly held doctrine or practice in the church.

Blessed are they which are persecuted for righteousness' sake: for theirs is the kingdom of heaven.

Blessed are ye, when men shall revile you, and persecute you, and shall say all manner of evil against you falsely, for my sake.

Rejoice, and be exceeding glad: for great is your reward in heaven: for so persecuted they the prophets which were before you.

Matthew 5

Six of Swords

THIS CARD DEPICTS A man steering a boat carrying passengers and six swords, across a body of water.

It could mean distancing yourself from a problem to gain objectivity, or taking time away for prayer and reflection. I am also reminded of Jesus's instructions to his disciples, that if their teaching was rejected in one place, to wipe the dust from their feet and move on to the next town.

If in combination with the Hierophant, as with the previous example, it could mean leaving that particular church or denomination. It could also signify leaving behind a job or position that conflicts with your faith.

Seven of Swords

IN THIS CARD, WE SEE the Fool returning from battle with several swords, some on the ground where his opponents have abandoned them.

This is a narrowly won battle, with gains and losses, perhaps. It may be that the principles you are living by are unpopular in your society and you have met with strong opposition.

Justice is turned back, and righteousness stands far away; for truth has stumbled in the public squares, and uprightness cannot enter.

Isaiah 59

In combination with a card like the Emperor or Empress, for example, it might mean living under a government whose policies don't reflect the teachings of Christ.

Eight of Swords

THIS CARD DEPICTS A woman in a barren place, bound and blindfolded, and surrounded by swords. She appears to be in peril, vulnerable, and unable to move.

She might have a lot of difficult situations and problems to resolve and feel overwhelmed or paralysed by indecision. The Eight of Swords also symbolises persecution because of one's beliefs.

If any of you lacks wisdom, you should ask God, who gives generously to all without finding fault, and it will be given to you.

James 1

Nine of Swords

IN THIS CARD, A WOMAN is shown sitting in bed, crying. Nine swords are above her on the wall. As the image suggests, you might be coping with many peoples problems or situations.

Combined with the Tower card, for example, it could mean praying for guidance in responding to a crisis or natural disaster.

O thou afflicted, tossed with tempest, and not comforted, behold, I will lay thy stones with fair colours, and lay thy foundations with sapphires.

Isaiah 54

Ten of Swords

THE CARD SHOWS A WOMAN, in a storm at sea, barely clinging to a rock, and surrounded by swords.

The tens in all the suits are generally thought to represent completion, so they can be viewed as a final exam before going on to the court cards.

In this card, the woman is in great peril, but she has found a rock to hold onto, and she is clinging for dear life.

When the storms of life have overwhelmed you, cling to the Rock. If you are experiencing heartbreak or rejection, for the sake of doing the right thing, you are blessed.

Trust in the Lord forever, for the Lord God is an everlasting rock.

Isaiah 26

Blessed are the pure in heart: for they shall see God.

Blessed are the peacemakers: for they shall be called the children of God.

The Lord is my rock, and my fortress, and my deliverer;

The God of my rock; in him will I trust: he is my shield, and the horn of my salvation, my high tower, and my refuge, my saviour; thou savest me from violence.

When the waves of death compassed me, the floods of ungodly men made me afraid;

The sorrows of hell compassed me about; the snares of death prevented me;

In my distress I called upon the Lord, and cried to my God: and he did hear my voice out of his temple, and my cry did enter into his ears.

2 Samuel 22

Page of Swords

THIS CARD SHOWS A YOUNG person holding a sword. This Page is in training to be a Knight of Swords. This might represent a person who is studying theology, law diplomacy, or any of the social sciences.

Knight of Swords

THIS IS A PERSON WHO works for the protection of society, in law enforcement, or social work, for example.

Queen/King of Swords

THIS IS SOMEONE WHO has mastered the Swords, and can govern effectively in this area. Judges, senators, administrators, ministers, and professors might be examples. This person has integrity, and is able to stand their ground in matters of ethics and human rights, not corrupted by power or swayed by popular opinion, false doctrine, or sentimentality. They make fair judgements and appropriate sentences. This is someone who will do the right thing in the face of great opposition, and whose arguments are reasoned and logical.

Cups

Cups represent love. Historically, it was a time of romance and chivalry, courtship, poetry and art, celebrating love. Cups can refer to romantic love or agape love. The cards are also thought to symbolise the Eucharist, or to represent the indwelling of the Spirit.

Ace of Cups

THIS CARD SHOWS A HAND coming down from heaven , holding a cup. It represents compassion. You are beginning to see people with empathy, or the ability to put yourself in their shoes.

Two of Cups

THIS CARD DEPICTS A man and woman sharing two cups and represents courtship and romantic love. Partnership, mutual attraction, compatibility, union. This is mutual support and reciprocation.

Three of Cups

IN THIS CARD, THREE people are holding cups and dancing together. It represents celebration of a wedding or the birth of a child. Together with the Fool card, it might mean celebrating a baptism.

Likewise, I say to you, there is joy in the presence of the angels of God over one sinner who repents.

Luke 15

Four of Cups

HERE THE PERSON IS looking downcast at three cups which have been emptied and discarded. Above her is a hand from heaven, holding a full cup. This card symbolises despondency or self-pity . It can result from personal suffering, like a broken relationship, or from hardship in God's service.

Five of Cups

THIS CARD SHOWS A MAN with 5 cups, two which are upright and three that are empty. This card represents loss or bereavement. In those days, women commonly died in childbirth, and babies often did not survive infancy. At such times people often struggle to understand why God allows suffering and death. We need to be gentle with those who mourn.

The Lord is close to the brokenhearted and saves those who are crushed in spirit.

Psalm 34

Six of Cups

THIS CARD DEPICTS PEOPLE helping one another. It symbolises community, a supportive environment. This is recovery from loss, with the loving help of others. This is the neighbour who brings a casserole, and the friend who listens when you need to vent. This is sacrificing your time and energy to lift someone up. This is people working together to feed the hungry and care for the sick.

Seven of Cups

THIS CARD DEPICTS A woman with several cups to choose from. Choosing love for family over fame or fortune, for example. Sacrificing your own needs, dreams or ambitions to support another.

Whosoever will come after me, let him deny himself, and take up his cross, and follow me.

35 For whosoever will save his life shall lose it; but whosoever shall lose his life for my sake and the gospel's, the same shall save it.

Mark 8

Eight of Cups

This could represent burnout, or bitterness from giving and not receiving. Feeling like your efforts have been wasted.

And if you lend to those from whom you expect to receive, what credit is that to you? Even sinners lend to sinners to be repaid in full.

"Love your enemies! Do good to them. Lend to them without expecting to be repaid. Then your reward from heaven will be very great, and you will truly be acting as children of the Most High, for he is kind to those who are unthankful and wicked. Luke 6

Nine of Cups

THIS CARD SHOWS A PERSON who has lots of cups but he is not sharing them. This is abundance, or fulfillment, at the expense of others. This is gratifying one's own needs while others go without.

What does it profit, my brethren, if a man says he has faith but has not works? Can his faith save him? If a brother or sister is ill-clad and in lack of daily food, and one of you says to them, "Go in peace, be warmed and filled," without giving them the things needed for the body, what does it profit? So faith by itself, if it has no works, is dead.

James 2

Ten of Cups

IN THIS CARD WE SEE a community where everyone looks happy and contented. They are sharing in the harvest. The poor and weak are provided for, and nobody is going without.

Page of Cups

THIS IS A PERSON WHO is learning how to care for others. Training in nursing, for example.

Knight of Cups

THIS IS A PERSON WHO works at caring for the physical and emotional or spiritual needs of others. Nurses, doctors, counselors, chaplains, musician, artist, for example. This is also cooking, homemaking and childcare.

King/Queen of Cups

THIS CARD REPRESENTS mastery in providing for the needs of others. Nurturing, protection, healing. A government whose policies provide for the sick and disabled, poor, weak, the aged. This could represent a church or faith organisation that cares for the homeless, for example.

Wands

———

Wands represent enterprise, discovery, exploration. These were the exciting days of discovery of the New World. The nobility had grown up with tales of King Arthur and other medieval heroes, and perhaps dreamed of adventure.

A scriptural analogy can be seen in the story of Nehemiah, when he organised the rebuilding of Jerusalem.

Ace of Wands

THE CARD SHOWS A WAND coming down from God's hand. You have heard of a need somewhere, maybe a natural disaster, and you are inspired to help.

And I asked them concerning the Jews who escaped, who had survived the exile, and concerning Jerusalem. And they said to me, "The remnant there in the province who had survived the exile is in great trouble and shame. The wall of Jerusalem is broken down, and its gates are destroyed by fire."

As soon as I heard these words I sat down and wept and mourned for days, and I continued fasting and praying before the God of heaven.

Nehemiah 1

Two of Wands

THIS CARD SHOWS A MAN with two wands, looking out over a parapet. This is taking time to plan and prepare for any contingencies. Analysis, contemplation. Deciding how best to proceed.

So I went to Jerusalem and was there three days. Then I arose in the night, I and a few men with me. And I told no one what my God had put into my heart to do for Jerusalem. There was no animal with me but the one on which I rode. I went out by night by the Valley Gate to the Dragon Spring and to the Dung Gate, and I inspected the walls of Jerusalem that were broken down and its gates that had been destroyed by fire.

Nehemiah 1

Three of Wands

THIS CARD REPRESENTS growth and expansion, a venture showing early signs of success. Finding like-minded people to join the venture.

I told them of the hand of my God that had been upon me for good, and also of the words that the king had spoken to me. And they said, "Let us rise up and build." So they strengthened their hands for the good work.

Nehemiah 2

Four of Wands

THE FOUR OF WANDS SYMBOLISES stability, and celebration for having achieved a goal. This is having support and resources to accomplish the task.

Five of Wands

THIS CARD REPRESENTS conflict and opposition, lack of teamwork, disputes about how to get things done. Disagreement, working at cross purposes.

Now when Sanballat heard that we were building the wall, he was angry and greatly enraged, and he jeered at the Jews. And he said in the presence of his brothers and of the army of Samaria, "What are these feeble Jews doing? Will they restore it for themselves? Will they sacrifice? Will they finish up in a day? Will they revive the stones out of the heaps of rubbish, and burned ones at that?"

Nehemiah 4

Six of Wands

THE SIX OF WANDS CARD depicts a person with 6 wands being celebrated. It signifies success, accolades and achievement, and giving credit where credit is due. When we are in the limelight there is a danger of pride.

Seven of Wands

TAKING A DEFENSIVE stand against opposition. Maybe people or circumstances are hindering your progress in some way.

From that day on, half of my servants worked on construction, and half held the spears, shields, bows, and coats of mail. And the leaders stood behind the whole house of Judah, who were building on the wall. Those who carried burdens were loaded in such a way that each labored on the work with one hand and held his weapon with the other. And each of the builders had his sword strapped at his side while he built.

Nehemiah 4

Eight of Wands

THIS CARD SHOWS SWIFT progress, trying to meet a deadline while facing opposition.

So we labored at the work, and half of them held the spears from the break of dawn until the stars came out.

Nehemiah 4

Nine of Wands

THIS IS PERSEVERANCE, meeting obstacles and overcoming them. Not giving up.

For they all wanted to frighten us, thinking, "Their hands will drop from the work, and it will not be done." But now, O God, strengthen my hands.

Nehemiah 6

Ten of Wands

HERE THE PROJECT HAS been completed, in spite of obstacles. Well done!

So the wall was finished on the twenty-fifth day of the month Elul, in fifty-two days. And when all our enemies heard of it, all the nations around us were afraid and fell greatly in their own esteem, for they perceived that this work had been accomplished with the help of our God.

Nehemiah 6

Page of Wands

A PERSON WHO IS STUDYING to be a paramedic, firefighter or in the military.

Knight of Wands

A PERSON WHO WORKS as an entrepreneur, or as a paramedic, firefighter, soldier.

Queen / King of Wands

THIS PERSON IS SUITED to lead in areas that require courage and creativity. In medieval times this might have been an explorer. This is also engineers, foreign affairs, disaster relief, coming to the aid of refugees.

Pentacles

Lay not up for yourselves treasures upon earth, where moth and rust doth corrupt, and where thieves break through and steal: but lay up for yourselves treasures in heaven

Matthew 6

Pentacles represent money, resources and worldly possessions. Some spiritual leaders will tell you that if you are a good person God will bless you with money, but worldly success is not a measure of godliness.

Verily I say unto you, That a rich man shall hardly enter into the kingdom of heaven. And again I say unto you, It is easier for a camel to go through the eye of a needle, than for a rich man to enter into the kingdom of God.

Matthew 6

Ace of Pentacles

THIS CARD SHOWS A HAND coming from heaven, bearing a pentacle. Its represents a gift of money, skills or resources. This is God's providence.

So don't worry. Don't say, 'What will we eat?' Or, 'What will we drink?' Or, 'What will we wear?' People who are ungodly run after all those things. Your Father who is in heaven knows that you need them. But put God's kingdom first. Do what he wants you to do. Then all those things will also be given to you.

Matthew 6

Two of Pentacles

THIS CARD SHOWS A PERSON juggling two pentacles. It symbolises deciding how best to use our resources effectively in serving others.

For which of you, desiring to build a tower, does not first sit down and count the cost, whether he has enough to complete it? Otherwise, when he has laid a foundation and is not able to finish, all who see it begin to mock him, saying, 'This man began to build and was not able to finish.'

Luke 14

Three of Pentacles

THIS CARD DEPICTS A woman with three pentacles, doing handwork. It illustrates using one's gifts or talents in a meaningful way.

Tell the righteous that it shall be well with them, for they shall eat the fruit of their deeds.

Isaiah 3

Four of Pentacles

THIS CARD REPRESENTS financial stability, where perhaps you are debt free and able to grow your resources.

Then he said to them, "Watch out! Be on your guard against wanting to have more and more things. Life is not made up of how much a person has."

Luke 12

Five of Pentacles

THIS CARD DEPICTS A warmly lit church, but outside, a woman and child, cold and destitute. The people within the church are well provided for, but are doing nothing for the poor.

Suppose a brother or a sister has no clothes or food. Suppose one of you says to them, "Go. I hope everything turns out fine for you. Keep warm. Eat well." And suppose you do nothing about what they really need. Then what good have you done?

James 2

Six of Pentacles

This card represents charity, and also paying fair wages to your employees. We are not to gain wealth at the expense of others misfortune.

You rich people, listen to me. Cry and weep, because you will soon be suffering. Your riches have rotted. Moths have eaten your clothes. Your gold and silver have lost their brightness. Their dullness will be a witness against you. Your wanting more and more will eat your body like fire. You have stored up riches in these last days. You have even failed to pay the workers who mowed your fields. Their pay is crying out against you. The cries of those who gathered the harvest have reached the ears of the Lord. He rules over all.

James 5

Seven of Pentacles

THIS CARD DENOTES STEADY work resulting in financial growth, an investment bearing fruit.

Dishonest money dwindles away, but he who gathers money little by little makes it grow. Proverbs 13

Eight of Pentacles

THE EIGHT OF PENTACLES symbolises rapid growth, discipline, and hard work. Maybe too much emphasis on gaining money.

No one can serve two masters at the same time. You will hate one of them and love the other. Or you will be faithful to one and dislike the other. You can't serve God and money at the same time.

Matthew 6

Nine of Pentacles

THIS IS HARVEST, WHEN there needs to be fair exchange of goods. It is also providing for the poor and for the future needs of the community, by taxation, for example.

When you reap the harvest of your land, do not reap to the very edges of your field or gather the gleanings of your harvest. Leave them for the poor and for the foreigner residing among you. I am the Lord your God.

Leviticus 23

Ten of Pentacles

This card denotes financial security, abundance, sharing resources, a healthy community in which everyone is provided for.

Master, you gave me two bags of silver to invest, and I have earned two more.'

"The master said, 'Well done, my good and faithful servant. You have been faithful in handling this small amount, so now I will give you many more responsibilities. Let's celebrate together!'

Matthew 25

Page of Pentacles

THIS IS A PERSON STUDYING to learn finance, business, or economics, for example.

Knight of Pentacles

THIS CARD DENOTES SOMEONE who works in finance, business or economics, for example.

Queen/King of Pentacles

THIS CARD SYMBOLISES a person in leadership who directs the financial affairs of a community. This is mastery in matters of business or finance. This is integrity, incorruptibility, and fiscal responsibility for the people in their care.

Using Tarot for Spiritual Practice

One method of using the cards for spiritual practice is the following:

Shuffle the cards, and then draw and lay out the cards, face up, until you get a Major card, and then stop. Place the major card above the others.

The minor cards represent the details of what is going on in your life, and the major card signifies the lesson behind the scenes.

For example, the Ace of Pentacles combined with the Lovers card, might signify that the person has received a gift of money or resources, enabling them to become financially stable so that in future they can get married and provide for a family.

The Ace of Pentacles in combination with the Chariot, could mean receiving money to be used for helping someone in need.

The Knight of Cups, together with the Death card, could denote studying to minister to people in hospice, for example.

Any card combined with the Fool card, would indicate that repentance is needed, and a fresh start in that area.

Remember that these are random cards, and may or may not not apply to your situation. They are a tool for illustrating spiritual truths, and not for predicting the future.

Best wishes on your faith journey.

Now the God of hope fill you with all joy and peace in believing, that ye may abound in hope, through the power of the Holy Spirit.

NANCY VIVIEN BLICQ

Romans 15

About the Author

The author is fellow believer who spent many years serving as a community chaplain.

She is also published on Quora.